The Little Book of Big Emotions

"Kids Have Feelings Too"

The Poems & Drawings of Bird Collier
(and friends)

CONTENTS

Kid Problems

"What are you so stressed about?"
My teacher always asks
You've got no bills or worries,
You're free to play and laugh
You have no job or boss
to answer to each day
I simply cannot understand
the frown that's on your face

But he's not on the playground
When I'm left out of games
He doesn't hear the snickers
When they mispronounce my name

He doesn't know the lunch lady says my account is due
And I will not be getting lunch if mom can't pay it soon
He doesn't know my favorite bike was taken from my yard
I asked dad for a new one but he says it will be hard

Plus I miss my Granpa Joe
We lost him just last year
He always took me fishing
And now he's just not here

It's so hard to understand
when someone says to me
A kid's life is so easy
Why don't you feel happy

Sometimes I do feel sad
And sometimes I am scared
And sometimes I don't know how I feel
I just need you to be there

So if you don't know what to say
To make me feel okay
Just lay here 'til I fall asleep
Tomorrow's a new day

5

Share???

I like it, I love it, it's mine
I play with it all of the time

You don't even know how to hold it
You're definitely not s'posed to throw it

No, taking turns does not sound good
I'd buy you your own right now if I could

Hey stop that! Try not to shake it
I'll cry for a week if you break it

Don't drop it, don't roll it, don't fly it...
Oh is that YOUR new toy? Can I try it?

Cavities: A Haiku

Candy is so good
Why can't I always have it
Oh yea, the dentist

Fart

What's the big deal mom?
The word is so fun to say
Wind isn't even something that can be broken anyway

It's not a basketball
That I would like to pass
But If I tell my mother that she says I'm giving sass

It's not a trumpet or trombone
Though I'll admit it is not mute
Yet still I cannot gather why you'd want to call it a toot

I took my time in crafting it
To me it's a work of art
So just this one time, please mama, I'd like to call it a...

Grand

She's warm and soft and smooth
With cushy curves and wrinkled grooves

I love to eat her cooking
And the candy she slips me when mom's not looking

The two best things on earth
Are sitting in her lap & digging through her purse

She gives the greatest hugs
She smells like pie and love

She always understands
There's no one like my Grand.

The Big Move

I'm tucked away under my bed
And I wish I had cleaned here like mama said

'Cause dust is getting in my nose
But if I sneeze then they will know

Exactly where to find me
Which is not the goal of hiding

So I'll cover my face and hold my breath
Until the moving van has left

Then they'll have to say
Okay, we won't go! We will stay

So you don't have to leave your friends
Or figure out how to start over again

At a new school, in a new place
Where it's possible no one will want to play

With a kid they know nothing about
So I'm staying put 'til they drag me out

Still I really wish I hadn't parked
Myself in a hiding place this dark

And now I can smell all the fixins
On the pizza they're all eating in the kitchen

I can hear my sad stomach growl
I bet I've been under here for half of an hour

Maybe moving won't be so bad
Maybe I'm overreacting a tad

I think I'll just go downstairs
A big slice of pizza might ease my fears

Practice

I hate it I hate it I do
I've been sitting here maybe an hour or two

Just trying to learn this hard song
And still I am getting like half the notes wrong

My fingers don't listen
They just cramp and stiffen
Why must I practice so long

Okay Okay I will try
But If I get it wrong there's a good chance I'll cry

It's hard to learn something new
I get so frustrated I don't know what to do

Oh wait there it goes
I just played every note
I'm the world's best pianist it's true!

In the dark

The monster in the dark has jagged teeth,
plus an extra arm, and it's coming for me

It won't get me if I play dead,
So I pull the covers up over my head

I peek out and Ah! It's still there.
Should I stay here or make a fast break for the stairs?

If I can just get myself to mom and dad's bed,
They can run in and chop off the big monster's head

I cannot just sit here and not do a thing,

So I scream for my mom and I hear her running

She sprints into my room, her robe is flying
My goodness she looks just as scared as I am

She turns on the light so we both can see
What it is that is scaring me

Oh would you look at that, it's just my coat and hat
Every once in a while I can overreact

Uh oh

The monster might have been more safe
Than the look that is on my mother's face

CRUSH

Not the one that's on the can
The one that wants to hold their hand

No, not the tiny chips of ice
The one you dream of every night

Not people packed into a tiny room
The one you want to give the moon

Not the one that tears you apart
The one that speeds your racing heart

I can't explain the feeling right
It's like my chest feels really tight

And every sound feels like a song
That makes me want to sing along

It's hard to breathe or try to relax
I can't even remember how I should act

Oh no! Is that her headed this way???
Help me! What do you think I should say?

(Oh LOOK HE'S RUN AWAY)

No Thanks: A Haiku

I do not want to
Kiss Aunt Margaret's hairy cheek
So please don't make me

PRESSURE

How do I say no

When they want me to say yes?

And how do I just walk away

Without looking scared to death?

How do I say stop

When no one wants me to?

Everyone will look at me

Like I'm some kind of fool.

How can I learn to speak up

Loud enough to hear over the din?

And how can I be myself

When myself doesn't quite fit in?

It's hard when I know what's right

And what my heart wants me to do

But others like doing wrong

And I want them to like me too.

I guess I can push my chin up

And straighten out my spine

And tell them I won't just go along

With whatever they're planning this time

Because people come and go

These friendships may not always be

But one thing is for certain

I'll always have to live with me.

BOOOOORED

I CAN'T SAY IT OUT LOUD, WITHOUT GETTING A CHORE
BUT THE TRUTH OF THE MATTER IS I'M VERY BORED

NOTHING GOOD ON THE TELLY, NOTHING FUN IN MY ROOM
I'VE USED UP EVERY TOY AND WATCHED EVERY CARTOON

I'VE READ EVERY BOOK IN THE HOUSE I SWEAR
I'VE COLORED AND DRAWN AND PLAYED SOLITAIRE

I'VE GONE OUTSIDE AND THEN COME BACK IN
I'VE RIDDEN MY BIKE AND GONE FOR A SWIM

THERE IS ABSOLUTELY LITERALLY NOTHING TO DO
CAN NO ONE ELSE SEE WHAT I AM GOING THROUGH?

AND THINGS WOULDN'T BE SO BLEAK TODAY
IF DAD HADN'T TAKEN MY TABLET AWAY

Invisible

I hate when kids are choosing 'cause
I always get picked last

And my teacher never names me as line
leader for the class

At first I thought it was my fault since I
am not the boldest

But even when I raise my hand no one
seems to notice

I asked my mom what I should do, I'm
tired of feeling lonely

She sat with me and held my hand and
this is what she told me

We wrap you in our love at home be-
cause the world is tough

There will be days you give your all and
still it's not enough

Some people will not understand the
brilliance of your star

But the people meant to bless your life
will love you as you are

They'll see you even when you do not
raise or wave your hand

They'll hold you up and be your legs on
days you cannot stand

They'll see the thing inside you that
connects your heart to theirs

They'll know just what to say to calm
you when you're feeling scared

These people they're your tribe and
they may take some time to find

The best way to attract them is to make
sure you are kind

And while you're looking for them, they
are looking for you too

They're talking to their moms right now
about their day at school

They also feel alone at times and wish
they had good pals

They hate to feel invisible and hate to
feel left out

So focus on your family now who loves
you come what may

Your tribe will find you soon enough
and you'll be on your way!

Sometimes we think that people who
are popular are happy

And that their lives are easier, their days
are never crappy

But things can be deceiving from the
outside looking in

You can be chosen first, and lead the
line, but not have one TRUE friend.

So take your time and be yourself even
if it is not fast

The friendships that come naturally are
the ones that always last.

Excitement

Ahhhhh!
There's lightening running up my back
And dynamite in my skin
I want to run and scream out loud
I can't even hold it in

My daddy says we're going out
To do my favorite thing
My heart starts beating triple time
My ears begin to ring

I'm trying to be patient but
Let's go dad, on the double!
My mom says if we don't leave soon
I'll probably get in trouble

Oh gosh this happens every time
He shouldn't have let me know
I think I'd better simmer down
Before I don't get to go

Me

Too big, too small, too round
Too short, too tall, too brown
Too pale, too thin, too long
Too freckled, too wrinkled, too strong
On any given day
Someone has something to say
But I'm too confident to be
Anything other than ME

Gone

Dad I have a question
Can you please make it plain
You always have the answers
That help relieve my pain

One day we were all together
Then suddenly bad days came
Our lives were all turned upside down
And nothing was ever the same

You always told us all to trust
That family is family forever
But if that is the case
Then why aren't we all still together

How can someone get sick
And go to the doctor for fixing
The doctor does all that they can do
And still that person's now missing

Gone from the dinner table
Gone from the swing in the yard
Gone from our morning prayer routine
I'm trying to be strong but it's hard.

When someone goes away
They leave a big empty space
Even if they have, like you say
Arrived in a better place

I don't know much about life
Since I haven't been here that long
I know that no one lives forever
But I can't believe that they're gone

Silver Lining: A Haiku

Mom and Dad Split Up
I'm sad and also confused
Do I get Christmas twice?

No is not an answer.

Explain it one more time.
I think I am still lost.
It's not about my feelings?
And not about the cost?

I cannot understand.
My mind cannot compute.
I am still mommy's baby boy.
I know I am still cute.

Maybe I asked too quickly.
I'll try again, but slow.
'Cuz there just is no way
That you're telling me NO.

Imagine

I am floating
High above everything that bothers me

I am dreaming
Free from all the things that I don't like

I am flying
Nothing and no one can hold me down

I am invisible
My problems cannot find me

I am anywhere
I travel on the wind to my favorite place

Inside my mind,
worlds appear and I am their greatest hero

My favorite place to in the whole wide world
is my imagination

The They

They say I am bossy
Because I know the rules

They say I'm a know-it-all
When I answer first in school

They say I'm a baby
Because I cried when Mufasa died

They say I'm too shy
When I hold all my feelings inside.

I think it won't matter
Whatever I do or say

I have to be the me I am
I can't worry about THEY.

Around

Mom told me to stop
But I love to spin around
Now I've lost my lunch

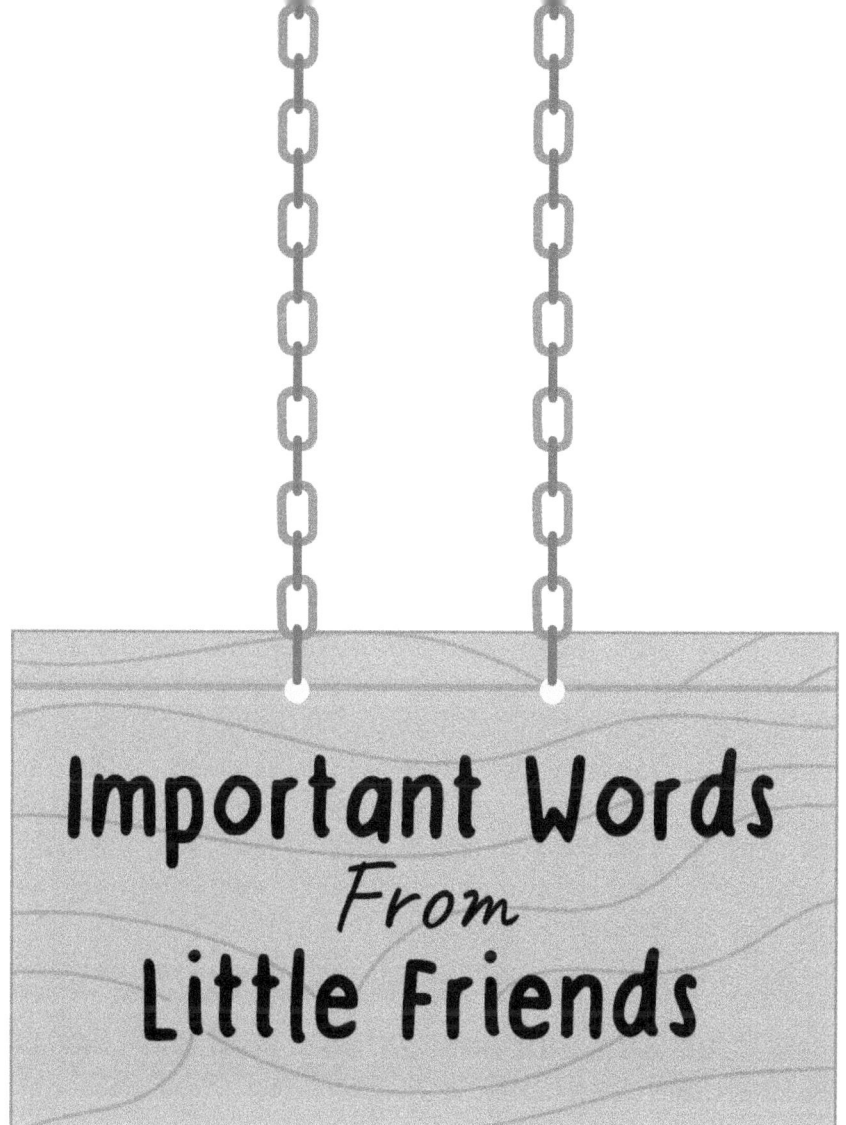

Important Words From Little Friends

Up, Down, and In Between

Author: Abigail E. Hill 9yo

Sometimes you feel up or down or in between,
Joyful, Doubtful, Mindless, and Mean.

Sometimes your energy boosts up high,
Which feels completely different when you're telling a lie.

I am sure you don't like it when you're down,
Feeling sad, wearing a frown.

Now, it is time to turn the frown into a smile,
A trip to the store has outfits with a brand, new style!

Please try and stay away from anger,
If you're not careful, it could lead to danger.

Next time you feel up, down, or in between,
It's your choice to be nice or mean.

Calm

Author: Jayce Collier 9yo

Calming like the ocean and sand.
The brightest blue, the sky so grand.
Sit and listen to the trees.
Feel the cooling summer breeze.
When the day turns into night,
The sky will fill with purple light.
You hear the sweet cicada's song
The feeling of calm is my favorite of all.

Happy

Author: Jayce Collier

It makes me want to fly not cry.
Happy is there even when you lose the race.
To cheer on your friend and be a good teammate.
Happy...mmmmm, like cake.

Mad

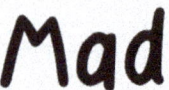

Author: Journey Collier 9yo

Being sad sometimes makes you mad
When you don't really want to cry.

And sometimes you can't get it out
Even if you really try.

Being mad is like anger filing a bubble
If you don't try to bring it down you will get into trouble

I Love the Fall

By Chandler Lightner 9yo

The trees are blowing
The wind is growing
It's cold outside
I'm warm inside
The leaves are falling
The birds are calling
I love the fall

Everyone Can Be a Poet

Writing poems can be fun. Poems don't always have rules. You can take whatever you are feeling and spread it out all over the page. You can tell the paper that you are sad and it won't make fun of you. You can tell the paper that you have a secret, and the paper won't go tell a friend. When you write you have a chance to search for the words that are the best match your feelings.

Sometimes that means you get to look up and learn new words. Other times you can find a new meaning in words you already know.

Do you want to practice. Come on! It will be fun. Use the blank page to write a poem. Think about your favorite place in the whole wide world. Now write down how you feel when you are in that place. Use as many or as few words as you want. Then give your poem a title.

Title: _____

A Poem by: _____

Title:

A Poem by:

Title:
A Poem by:

Title:
A Poem by:

Title:

A Poem by:

Title:

A Poem by:

Title:

A Poem by:

Title:

A Poem by:

Title:
A Poem by: